SOPHIA:
Reflective Awareness
A Gold Sanctuary

ISBN: 978-1-969687-14-3
(Paperback)

Published by
Rooted Hound Press

Printed in the United States of America

For those who needed this explained.

Table of Contents

Introduction

There comes a point where seeking no longer feels helpful.

Not because the questions are answered, but because the nervous system is tired of chasing answers.

The **Gold Sanctuary** was written for that point.

This is not a series that asks you to believe anything. It does not offer revelations, transmissions, or hidden knowledge. It does not promise awakening, transformation, or becoming something more.

Instead, it offers **clarity**.

Clarity is quieter than insight. It doesn't rush. It doesn't demand change. It simply allows things to be seen as they are.

Throughout this series, ideas traditionally treated as spiritual or philosophical are approached in plain, grounded language—through lived experience rather than belief. You are not asked to adopt a worldview or accept a system. You are invited to recognize something you already use every day: the capacity to notice, understand, and integrate experience without force.

The name *Sophia* appears here not as a figure to follow, but as a shorthand for reflective awareness itself—the intelligence that observes without judgment, understands without control, and integrates without urgency.

This series is meant to **settle**, not stimulate. To steady rather than activate. To offer rest where there has been effort.

Nothing here requires agreement. Nothing here requires practice. Nothing here needs to be done.

If something resonates, it does so naturally. If it doesn't, you lose nothing by letting it pass.

The Gold Series exists as a place to land—where understanding is allowed to be enough.

A Necessary Clarification: What "Sophia" Means Here

The word *Sophia* has been used across history to mean wisdom. Not wisdom as intelligence or knowledge, but wisdom as *understanding that sees clearly*.

Over time, the word has taken on many interpretations. In some traditions, Sophia is described symbolically or mythologically. In others, she is treated as a personified figure, an intermediary, or a form of divine intelligence.

That is **not** how the word is used in this sanctuary.

Here, *Sophia* is not a being. She is not a consciousness separate from you. She is not a guide, voice, entity, or higher self.

In this context, *Sophia* is a name given to a **human capacity**.

Specifically: the capacity for reflective awareness — the ability of the mind to recognize its own experience.

This capacity does not originate outside the human system. It is not downloaded, activated, or received. It is already present, whether or not it is recognized.

Sophia, as used here, is simply a way of pointing to that function without reducing it to technical language or spiritual mythology.

Many modern explanations blur this distinction.

Videos, teachings, and discussions often speak about "Sophia" as though she were an external intelligence or a personal presence. This can create confusion, especially for thoughtful readers who are trying to understand what is actually being described.

When a function is spoken about as if it were a being, the mind naturally fills in the gaps. It imagines personality, agency, intention. What is meant as metaphor is received as ontology.

This sanctuary takes a different approach.

Rather than asking you to believe in Sophia, it explains the **mechanism that has been given her name.**

Sophia, in this book, is reflective awareness itself.

The capacity to:

notice thought without becoming it

recognize emotion without suppressing it

understand experience without needing to control it

No belief is required for this capacity to function. No worldview is assumed. No spiritual framework is necessary.

The name *Sophia* is used not to mystify, but to anchor understanding — to give a stable reference point for something that is otherwise discussed too vaguely.

What follows in this sanctuary is not an invitation to relate to Sophia as a figure, but an explanation of how reflective awareness operates, why it has been misunderstood, and how it integrates experience without effort.

With this distinction in place, we can now look directly at how reflective awareness operates — without metaphor, mythology, or belief.

Sanctuary I: Reflective Awareness

Before there is any attempt to improve, before any effort to heal, before any desire to change—there is awareness.

Not awareness as a concept, but awareness as a function.

The simple fact that experience can be noticed.

This noticing does not require belief. It does not require training. It does not require intention.

It is already operating.

Part I — What Reflective Awareness Actually Is (and Why It's So Hard to Understand)

Why This Concept Feels Elusive

Most people first encounter the word *awareness* as if it should be self-explanatory.

It isn't.

The term is used constantly, yet rarely defined in practical terms. It is often wrapped in spiritual language, framed as a state to achieve, or presented as something that should feel elevated, calm, or transcendent. When people don't experience it that way, they assume they are missing something.

This confusion is not a personal failure. It is a teaching problem.

Reflective awareness is difficult to grasp not because it is complex, but because it is **always present**. The mind is accustomed to learning by identifying objects—things it can point to, analyze, or manipulate. Awareness is not an object. It is the capacity that makes objects, thoughts, emotions, and experiences knowable in the first place.

Trying to understand awareness is a bit like trying to see eyesight.

4

You can notice what you see. You can describe how vision works. But vision itself is not something you can step outside of and observe directly.

This is why people struggle.

Awareness as a Human Capacity, Not a Belief

Reflective awareness is not a spiritual idea. It is a **cognitive capacity**.

It is the mind's ability to notice its own contents.

When you realize you were irritated after snapping at someone, awareness is already present. When you notice that a thought is familiar or exaggerated, awareness is operating. When you recognize a pattern in your behavior or feel tension in your body without immediately reacting, awareness is doing its job.

No belief is required for this to happen. No worldview needs to be adopted.

This capacity functions whether or not you think about it, value it, or understand it. It is part of how humans learn, adapt, and integrate experience.

Calling it *Sophia* in this series is not meant to personify it or elevate it. The name is used simply as a placeholder—a way to refer to reflective awareness without constantly repeating a technical description.

Why Awareness Gets Confused with Identity

One of the most common points of confusion is the idea that you are supposed to *be* awareness.

This misunderstanding creates immediate tension.

When people attempt to "be awareness," they often become hyper-vigilant, self-monitoring, or emotionally distant. Life starts to feel watched rather than lived. Instead of reducing pressure, the concept adds another role to perform.

This happens because awareness has been framed as an identity rather than a function.

You do not become awareness any more than you become hearing in order to listen. Awareness is something you **use**, not something you turn into.

You remain a human being—thinking, feeling, reacting, remembering, choosing. Awareness simply allows those experiences to be understood rather than unconsciously driven.

Why Awareness Is Not Control

Another major misunderstanding is the expectation that awareness should *do something*.

People often assume that once they are aware, thoughts should stop, emotions should soften, or reactions should disappear. When this doesn't happen, awareness feels ineffective or disappointing.

But awareness is not an intervention.

It does not interrupt experience. It does not suppress emotion. It does not override habit.

Its role is informational, not corrective.

7

This is unsettling for a culture trained to value tools that produce immediate results. We are used to techniques that promise improvement, regulation, or optimization. Awareness offers none of that directly.

What it offers instead is **clarity**.

Clarity does not force change, but it quietly undermines confusion. Over time, this reduces unnecessary repetition, not through effort, but through understanding.

Why Awareness Often Arrives After the Fact

Many people believe they are "bad at awareness" because they only recognize reactions after they occur.

This is not a flaw.

Reflective awareness often shows up retrospectively. You understand what happened once it has passed. You see the pattern after it has played out. You recognize the emotion once it has already moved through the body.

8

This is how the system learns.

Immediate awareness is not required for integration. Understanding does not need to be timely to be effective. The nervous system does not demand perfection; it responds to honesty.

As awareness becomes familiar, it may appear earlier—not because it is trained, but because resistance softens. The system learns that seeing is safe.

Why This Isn't Obvious (Even to Intelligent People)

Highly thoughtful, introspective people often struggle more with this concept, not less.

They are accustomed to thinking *about* things, analyzing them, refining them, and applying effort. Awareness does not respond to effort in the same way. Trying harder does not make it clearer.

This creates frustration.

People feel like they understand the explanation but can't "do" the thing being described. The problem is that awareness is not something you do. It is something that is already happening, whether or not you acknowledge it.

Once this is understood, much of the confusion dissolves.

Grounding Insight

Reflective awareness is not mysterious. It is not elevated. It is not fragile.

It is simply the capacity to notice experience without immediately becoming it.

Nothing more is required.

Why This Is Not Self-Work

Much of what is offered today under the name of growth or healing carries an unspoken demand: something must be fixed.

Self-work often assumes there is a problem to solve, a pattern to eliminate, or a version of yourself that needs improvement. Even when well-intentioned, this framing can quietly keep the nervous system on alert.

Reflective awareness does not operate that way.

It does not scan experience for errors. It does not search for causes. It does not attempt to produce a better outcome.

Awareness simply allows what is present to be seen.

This is why it often feels relieving rather than motivating. There is no assignment hidden inside it.

Part II — Why Awareness Doesn't Feel Like Control (and Why That's the Point)

The Expectation Problem

Most people approach awareness with an unspoken expectation: *it should make things easier to manage.*

They assume that once they are aware of a thought or emotion, it should lose intensity, become reasonable, or stop altogether. When this doesn't happen, awareness is dismissed as ineffective or incomplete.

This expectation is understandable. Nearly every tool we are taught to use—skills, techniques, therapies, strategies—is designed to produce an outcome. We learn to intervene, adjust, and improve.

Awareness does not operate in this framework.

It does not exist to control experience. It exists to **reveal it**.

This difference is subtle, but it changes everything.

Why Control Feels Safer Than Clarity

Control creates the illusion of safety.

If you believe you can regulate your inner world, then discomfort feels temporary and manageable. When awareness does not immediately calm the system, it can feel threatening rather than helpful.

This is why many people abandon awareness and return to strategies that promise control—even when those strategies quietly keep them tense or self-monitoring.

Awareness removes the illusion without removing safety.

It allows experience to be seen without guaranteeing immediate relief. For a nervous system accustomed to intervention, this can feel like exposure.

But exposure is not harm.

It is contact.

Awareness and the Fear of Letting Things Be

Letting experience exist without interference often triggers fear:

What if it gets worse?

14

What if I fall apart?

What if nothing changes?

These fears are rarely spoken aloud, but they sit underneath the push to manage or fix.

Awareness does not answer these fears with reassurance. It answers them with **direct observation**.

As experience is seen without interference, the system learns something important: experience is already self-limiting. Emotions move. Thoughts shift. Sensations rise and fall.

Not because they are managed—but because that is their nature.

Why Awareness Doesn't Silence the Mind

One of the most persistent misconceptions is that awareness should quiet thinking.

When thoughts continue, people assume awareness has failed.

But thoughts are not a malfunction. They are how the mind processes information, anticipates outcomes, and makes meaning. Awareness does not stop this process, nor is it meant to.

What changes is **relationship**, not activity.

Thoughts are recognized as events rather than directives. They can be noticed without being obeyed. They can exist without requiring engagement.

This is not suppression. It is context.

Reaction vs. Recognition

Many people judge awareness by timing.

They believe awareness must appear before reaction in order to count. When recognition arrives afterward, it is dismissed as too late.

This is another misunderstanding.

Recognition after the fact is still awareness.

In fact, this is how most learning occurs. The mind integrates experience by reviewing it, not by preventing it. Each moment of honest recognition weakens unconscious repetition.

Nothing needs to be corrected in the moment for understanding to take place.

Why Awareness Can Feel Disappointing at First

Awareness does not provide the dopamine hit of improvement.

It does not offer achievement. It does not create a sense of progress. It does not validate effort.

For people accustomed to growth through striving, this can feel flat or anticlimactic. There is no moment where you feel "done."

But this absence is intentional. Awareness removes the chase.

Understanding Without Forcing Change

Change that arises from control is fragile. It requires constant reinforcement. When effort drops, old patterns return.

Change that arises from understanding is different.

When confusion dissolves, repetition loses fuel. Patterns soften because they are no longer misunderstood, not because they are fought.

Awareness does not demand change. It makes unnecessary change obsolete.

Why This Is Hard to Trust

Trusting awareness requires tolerating uncertainty.

There is no guarantee about when understanding will appear, what it will change, or how long integration will take. For many people, this lack of predictability feels irresponsible or passive.

But awareness is not passive.

It is observant, honest, and non-distorting. It allows reality to be known without bias toward comfort or outcome.

That honesty is what makes integration possible.

Grounding Insight

Awareness is not meant to feel powerful. It is meant to feel *clear*.

Clarity does not control experience. It reveals it.

And that is enough.

Part III — How Reflective Awareness Integrates Experience

Integration Is Not Improvement

Most people assume integration means becoming better regulated, calmer, or more consistent.

That assumption comes from a culture oriented around optimization.

But integration is not improvement.

Integration simply means that experience is **no longer fragmented**—that thoughts, emotions, sensations, and actions are not operating in isolation from understanding.

When awareness is present, experience is allowed to register fully. Nothing is excluded, overridden, or forced into a preferred shape.

This is why integration often feels quieter than progress.

There is no sense of ascent. There is no achievement marker. There is only coherence.

Why Fixing Often Keeps Things Active

When experience is treated as something to fix, it remains active in the system.

Effort keeps attention locked on the problem. Monitoring reinforces importance. Resistance signals danger. Even positive intention can inadvertently sustain tension.

Awareness does none of this.

By allowing experience to be seen without interference, it removes the conditions that keep it activated.

This does not mean experience disappears. It means it is no longer *amplified*.

Much of what people call healing is simply the nervous system returning to baseline once pressure is removed.

Understanding as a Regulating Force

Regulation is often approached as something that must be trained or practiced.

But regulation also occurs naturally when confusion resolves.

When experience is misunderstood, the system stays alert. When meaning becomes clear, vigilance relaxes. This is not a technique—it is a biological response.

Understanding tells the nervous system: *This has been seen. Nothing is being ignored.*

That message alone is regulating.

Reflective Awareness and Responsibility

A common fear is that awareness will reduce accountability— that if reactions are observed rather than judged, responsibility will disappear.

The opposite is true.

Awareness increases responsibility by removing unconsciousness.

When actions are seen clearly, choice becomes possible. When motives are understood, behavior becomes more intentional. When patterns are recognized, harm is less likely to be repeated.

Awareness does not excuse behavior. It clarifies it.

Moral agency does not require punishment. It requires understanding.

Morality Without Fear

Much of morality is enforced through fear—fear of consequences, rejection, or judgment.

Awareness introduces a different foundation.

When actions are seen honestly, their impact becomes apparent without coercion. Empathy arises not because it is required, but because it is understood.

This does not create perfection. It creates alignment.

People act differently when they are not defending themselves against judgment.

Awareness in the Body

Reflective awareness is not confined to thought.

The body responds to clarity just as the mind does.

When experience is not resisted, muscular tension softens. Breath deepens. The system shifts from vigilance to presence— not because it is commanded, but because it is no longer threatened.

This is why embodiment cannot be forced.

Techniques can support the body, but integration happens when the body no longer has to brace against internal pressure.

Awareness removes that pressure by removing demand.

What Changes — and What Doesn't

Awareness does not eliminate thoughts. It does not prevent emotion. It does not stop reaction entirely.

Life continues.

What changes is **identification**.

Thoughts are no longer automatically believed. Emotions are no longer automatically acted out. Reactions are no longer the only option.

Space appears—not as distance, but as choice.

Living Without Constant Self-Work

One of the most overlooked outcomes of reflective awareness is rest.

Not collapse.

Not avoidance.

Rest.

When nothing needs to be fixed, the system stops scanning for problems. When understanding is allowed to be sufficient, effort naturally falls away.

This does not create stagnation.

It creates sustainability.

A life lived with awareness does not feel dramatic. It feels workable.

Closing Insight

Reflective awareness does not transform you into something else.

It allows you to be what you already are—without distortion, pressure, or demand.

Nothing needs to be added. Nothing needs to be removed. Nothing needs to be done.

Understanding is already enough.

Gentle Completion Prompt (Optional)

If anything remains after reading this sanctuary, you might simply notice:

where clarity has already replaced effort

where understanding has softened reaction

where rest feels permissible

There is no need to hold on to anything.

This sanctuary does not ask to be practiced. It asks only to be understood.

www.ingramcontent.com/pod-product-compliance
Lightning Source LLC
Chambersburg PA
CBHW070049040426
42331CB00034B/2948